We care for God's Creation

written by Christine Way Skinner
illustrations by Céleste Gagnon

Catholic Kids' Library

Cover design, layout and illustrations: Céleste Gagnon

Published in Canada by Novalis

Publishing Office
1 Eglinton Avenue East, Suite 800
Toronto, Ontario, Canada
M4P 3A1

Head Office
4475 Frontenac Street
Montréal, Québec, Canada
H2H 2S2

en.novalis.ca

Cataloguing in Publication is available from Library and Archives Canada
ISBN: 978-2-89830-174-2

Published in the United States by

Twenty-Third Publications,
a division of Bayard, Inc.
977 Hartford Turnpike, Unit A
Waterford, CT 06385
(860) 437-3012 or (800) 321-0411
twentythirdpublications.com

ISBN: 978-1-62785-838-0

Printed in China.

We acknowledge the support of the Government of Canada.

Nihil Obstat: Monsignor Murray J. Kroetsch
Censor liborum
September 17, 2024

Imprimatur: Most Rev. Douglas Crosby, OMI
Bishop of Hamilton
September 17, 2024

5 4 3 2 1 29 28 27 26 25

We are part of a marvellous world
that God made out of great, great love.

Our planet Earth is in a universe so big
that even if we spent our whole life travelling
through it, we would see only a tiny part of it!

In the world God made, there is also life so small that we cannot see it with our bare eyes.

The world is full of so many different kinds of things.
There are thousands of kinds of flowers.

There are millions of kinds of animals and insects.

There are billions of people...
and no two are the same.

Every one of these is made by God,
is loved by God and is needed in the world.
And every one of them praises God
just by being what it is.

God is so great that many, many kinds of things are needed to praise God. Some creatures praise God with their voices... some praise God with their beauty...

… and some praise God by serving others so that others may live well.

The things God made also give praise by teaching us about who God is!

Rocky canyons and giant trees show us that God is strong and dependable.

Lilies and sparrows remind us that God takes great care of us, so we do not need to be afraid. Gentle breezes and soft grass help us know that God will comfort us when we are sad.

When we see a rainbow after the rain,
we can remember that God promises
to love us forever.

A tiny mustard seed can teach us that no matter how small we are, our good actions can grow... and grow... and grow.

All of these are God's works of art,
and God loves them all.

God asks people to care for
all of Creation and our common home.

God wants all people and every living thing in the world to have clean air to breathe, fresh water to drink and enough food to eat.

God asks us to take care of the air
and all that live in the air…

… the land and all that live on the land…

... the water and all that live in the water.

The air and the land and the water, and all the creatures that live in them, also take care of us.

Thanks to trees and other plants, the air gives us the breath of life...

... the land gives us food and shelter...

… and the water gives us something to drink and keeps us clean.

Each of us has been given gifts
to take care of our common home...

Some of us have the gift of curiosity and
will become scientists to learn about how
to live in peaceful ways with our planet...

Some of us have the gift of creativity and will become inventors to help make things that keep us and our common home safe.

And some of us have the gifts of caregiving and will become farmers or fishers and carefully tend the land and ocean.

What are your special gifts?
How can you help care for God's Creation?

Use less water

Attend an Earth Day event

Recycle

Plant a tree or garden

Pick up litter

Thank God for Creation!

The world God created is a marvellous gift.
It is a gift that needs our care and protection.
Let's care for our common home together!

Dear Parents and Caregivers

Foster a deep love for Creation and a sense of responsibility for our common home...

- **Lead by example:** Children learn by watching what we do. If our actions show that the created world is a sacred trust, they will develop a similar reverence for God's Creation.
- **Nurture wonder and awe:** When children follow the promptings of their curious eyes and ears, they encounter marvels we might otherwise miss. Spending time observing ants working atop their colony or a butterfly as it emerges from its chrysalis is worship if it leads to praise and thanksgiving. Children will also be inspired if we show reverence toward God's Creation.
- **Pray with an ecological heart:** Express gratitude for the gifts of the earth before meals. Rest on the Sabbath and reconnect with nature on the day of rest God gave to all Creation. Pray with natural symbols. Water, oil, fire, flowers and beeswax, wood and stone are symbols from the natural world that have spoken to humanity of aspects of the divine from the beginning of human consciousness and are used in liturgy. Help children make the connection between these symbols of praise and reverence for Creation.
- **Make earth-friendly choices in your home:** Develop new eco-friendly habits. Avoid single-use plastics. Bring your own bags and water bottles. Give gifts of time and experiences rather than things. Plant a garden – even a small window box. Use natural cleaning products. Limit food waste by using leftovers in creative ways and portioning only what is likely to be eaten (including at buffet restaurants). Compost. Consider the climate when voting.
- **Nurture hope:** Hope motivates; fear paralyzes. While we need to be deeply concerned about the climate crisis, love for Creation and hope for the future are more likely to lead us to change our behaviour. Fear of climate disaster can lead to anxiety in children. If you or your children experience anxiety, look for resources to help you develop healthy coping strategies.
- **Learn:** The more we learn about our universe, the more we will see how miraculous it is. Read *Laudato Si'*, *Laudate Deum* and other Church documents on faith and ecology. Learn about Saint Francis of Assisi, the patron saint of ecology – you can even place a statue of him in your garden or a flowerpot. Pray his "Canticle of the Creatures."
- **Foster ecological virtues:** Tenderness, compassion, humility and concern for our fellow human beings, for other creatures and for the planet itself are just a few of the virtues we need to become better planetary citizens. Peace, justice and the preservation of the planet are all connected!